A FUNNY FEELING

A FUNNY FEELING

Poems by Richard S. Kimball

Drawings by William K. Reid, Jr.

Green Timber Publications
Portland, Maine

A FUNNY FEELING
Copyright © 1988 by Richard S. Kimball

All rights reserved. No part of this book may be reproduced in any form or by any electronic or mechanical means without permission in writing from the publisher, except in the case of brief quotations embodied in critical articles or reviews.

Published by Green Timber Publications,
P.O. Box 3884, Portland, Maine 04104

Library of Congress Cataloging-in-Publication Data

Kimball, Richard S., 1939-
  A funny feeling/poems by Richard S. Kimball; drawings by William K. Reid, Jr.
    p.   cm.
  Summary: An illustrated collection of forty-one poems describing different feelings and emotions.
  ISBN 0-944443-00-1
  1. Emotions--Juvenile poetry. 2. Children's poetry, American. [1. Emotions--Poetry. 2. American poetry.] I. Reid, William Kenneth, 1933-   ill. II. Title.
PS3561.I4166F85 1988
811'.54--dc 19   87-32155
                                                      CIP
                                                       AC

Dedication

to everybody who has ever had—or caused—a funny feeling

Contents

Foreword   11

A Funny Feeling   13
Shirley   14
Timothy   15
Deep Feelings   16
Nancy   18
Frances   19
Rod   20
Reginald   22
Dreams   23
Burt and Gail   24
Cynthia   25
The Weatherbees   26
Louise   27
Jeremy   28
Ruth Ann   29
Joan   30
Would You?   31
Hugh   33
Wrong   34
Bob   35
Lucille and Neal   36
Joe   37
Sam   38
Annie   39
Cindy Lou   40

How Far?   42
Barnaby   43
Feelingmore Farr   44
Sid   46
Whittington   47
Andrea   48
David Lee   49
Ed   51
Abigail   52
R. Larson Brown   53
Pamela and Frank   54
A Physical Feeling   55
Sue   56
Mortimer Sharp   58
Laurie   59
What Can You Do?   60

Foreword

Delivery room doctors traditionally lift newborn infants by the feet and give them gentle slaps. The idea is to clear passages and get the infants breathing on schedule. But the practice has a second important result. It mixes the infants' feelings up inside them and thus provides a realistic introduction to life with emotions.

Whether delivery room practice is the reason or not, most of us are destined to pass through life with sometimes mixed and sometimes funny feelings. This book is designed in part to help the reader feel comfortable with those feelings. But mostly it is designed for fun.

Enjoy.

A Funny Feeling

A funny feeling creeps and crawls beneath my skin.
What next? Will it come bubbling up and make me grin?
Or will it spread and hurt and make sad tears begin?
I wonder what this feeling is that sneaks within.

I know it can't be anger, because I am not mad.
It can't be sorrow either, because I am not sad.
And it is not sweet pleasure, because I am not glad.
This seems to be a feeling that I've never ever had.

But still this feeling feels a little old and used,
As if by bits of it I once have been amused,
Or if by other bits I once have been abused.
The whole, however, makes me a bit confused.

This is no simple feeling; it's a mixed-up mess,
A mangled mess of fear and joy and anxiousness,
A total jumbled mess, enough to cause, I guess,
A lot of other people deep distress.

Such confusing feelings, though, cause me no agony.
They never make me scream or race to climb a tree.
In fact I've learned to welcome them, because, you see,
These mixed up funny feelings help me know I'm me.

I'll let this strange familiar feeling lurk within,
So that my search to understand it can begin.
And when I do I'll feel it change beneath my skin
Into content and joy enough to make me grin.

Shirley

Surly Shirley lost her temper.
> So she tried to find it.

She stamped her feet to scare it from under the couch.
> It was not there.

She cried to make it return.
> It did not.

She screamed to see if it would answer.
> It did not.

Shirley's mother put her to bed, and Shirley pounded the pillow to see if her temper was hiding underneath.
> It was not.

When Shirley woke up, her temper was back.
> Shirley was pleased.

"Welcome back," she said.
> "Now I'll keep you where you belong."

Timothy

Timothy bottled his feelings all up.
    Whatever he felt, he would hide.
Most of his friends were quite different from him.
    They snorted, and giggled, and cried.
Timothy, though, was a stoical boy.
    He always remained dignified.

Then came a terrible, horrible day.
    It began when a bee stung his side.
Two other boys started laughing at him.
    They teased him and called him cross-eyed.
Next his new bicycle fell down and broke,
    And both of his goldfish died.
Timothy burned his poor tongue with pea soup,
    And saw that his shoe was untied.

Timothy's feelings just had to explode,
    No matter the cost to his pride.
Weeping and shouting, he said, "That's enough!"
    And blew all his tops far and wide.
Wave after wave of his feelings poured out;
    They seemed like a sea with a tide.

"Look at this mess," said his mother in awe,
    When Timothy's tears had dried.
"Please let your feelings come out bit by bit,
    And don't keep them bottled inside."

Deep Feelings

Deep-seated feelings don't come in a box,
    We can't find them in a drawer.
But they're always there to give us hard knocks
    Or to make our spirits soar.

Some feelings give us a pain in the head
    Or make our stomachs crawl.
But without any feelings, we would be dead
    So we have to feel them all.

Some feelings like hate we try to erase
    Unless we like to feel small.
And others like love we always embrace,
    For love feels best of them all.

Not all of our feelings can be understood,
    Some of them feel bizarre.
But even the feelings that hurt can be good—
    They help us be more than we are.

Feelings are meant to be more than just felt;
    They need a thoughtful reaction.
Then the best and the worst that we'll ever be dealt
    Can lead to satisfaction.

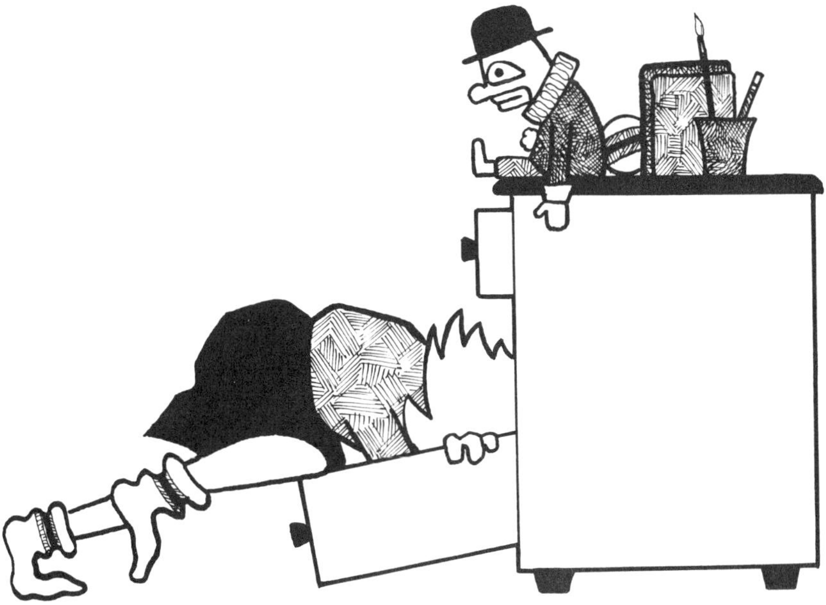

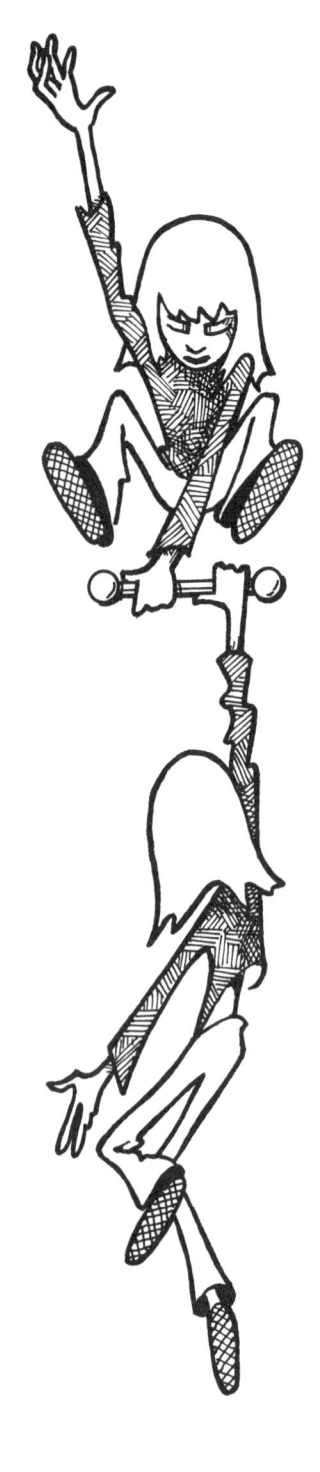

Nancy

Nancy had a handle on herself

When she felt
           low

Nancy grabbed the handle

           up
And lifted herself

           high
When she felt too

Nancy grabbed the handle

And pulled herself back
           down

When she took a wrong t u r n

Nancy grabbed the handle

And pulled herself a r o u n d

When she fell behind

Nancy grabbed the handle

And pulled herself a l o n g

Nancy had a handle on herself.

Frances

Frances couldn't have a cat
And she couldn't have a dog
So she got herself a peeve
And she took it everywhere.
"That's my pet peeve," she said
When Agnes snapped her gum.
"That's my pet peeve," she said
When Richard chewed his thumb.
"That's my pet peeve," she said
When Thomas acted dumb.
Frances loved her peeve
And paid more attention to it
Than she did to her friends.
Until her friends grew angry
And said to her,
"Your pet peeve is our pet hate,
So make it go away."
Frances thought a bit,
Then did just that.
She said "goodby" to the peeve
And got back friends instead.

Rod

Here's a story very odd
About a tiny boy named Rod
Who failed to make the football squad
Because he had a lightweight bod.

He said he didn't give a hoot
But then he hollered "darn" and "shoot"
And, acting like an angry brute,
He gave the ball a mighty boot.

The ball rose upward toward the sky.
Up it went, so far, so high,
That those who watched it saw it fly
Off into the by and by.

The coach said Rod could kick that fall
Despite the fact that he was small.
But now there was no team at all—
It could not play without a ball.

And that's why Rod won football fame
But never played a single game.

21

Reginald

Reginald Botts was tied up in knots.
        He could not get his thoughts undone.
His parents pulled at many spots,
        But could not get the knots undone.
The doctor tried some pills and shots,
        But could not get the thoughts undone.
His grandmother gave him lots and lots
        Of love. And got the knots undone.

"It's simple," she said, as she turned to her pots.
"That's why they call them granny knots."

Dreams

Dreams bring feelings in the night—
Sometimes of pleasure,
Sometimes of fright.
If the dream is a bad one,
Then reach for the light.
But if it's a good one,
Curl up and sleep tight.

Burt and Gail

The extrovert Burt
Wore his feelings like a shirt
With colors so bright
That they glowed in the night.

The introvert Gail
Wore her feelings like a snail
In a shell so thick
It was tougher than brick.

Burt was often so loud
He seemed like a crowd
Even standing alone
Or calling by phone.

Gail seemed to cower
So they called her "wallflower"
And "shrinking violet"—
She was easy to forget.

There seemed little hope
The two would ever cope
As a pair—but that was wrong
For they really got along.

When they met and broke the ice
They found each other nice.
These two strange mavericks
Together made a perfect mix.

Burt's light cast a spell
Which drew Gail from her shell,
And Gail's answering smile
Helped Burt calm his style.

So those who'd pull back
From her slack and his yack
Began to enjoy
Both girl and boy.

Cynthia

"Can't you think straight?" yelled Cynthia's dad,
When Cynthia's brother made her mad
And Cynthia hit the smart-mouthed lad.
"Learn to think straight! Don't be bad!"

Cynthia tried with grunts and stares
To straighten out her thoughts and cares,
But they zoomed off and climbed the stairs,
Then went to find her friendly bears.

With little brother in her view
(Who should be kicked with her hard shoe)
This thinking straight and thinking true
Was hard for Cynthia to do.

Her straightened thoughts met such bad ends
She gave those thoughts new curves and bends
And sent them into bedroom dens
Where they could snuggle with her friends.

The Weatherbees

When you go to visit the Weatherbees
First you will sweat and then you will freeze,
So take lots of clothes to the Weatherbees.

>Wilma Weatherbee has a temper so hot
>That she once melted a kitchen pot.
>
>Her brother Fred is so cucumber cool
>That he once iced up the swimming pool.
>
>Her mother has a sense of humor so dry
>That it can make their pet fish cry.
>
>Her father is such a huge windbag
>That curtains flap when he starts to brag.

In fact it is best—if you don't like to freeze
And then to sweat and then to sneeze—
To stay right away from the Weatherbees.

Louise

Louise heard Marianne
Ask Betsy Jo to a party
With Sam and Alice and Tom.
Louise grew so angry
At not being asked
That she picked up a grudge
And carried it around all day.
The grudge was larger than Louise.
It crunched her under its weight.
So when Marianne called
And asked her to come with Betsy Jo
And Sam and Alice and Tom,
Louise was forced to say no.
She had grown too small
To go out.

Jeremy

Jeremy's head is screwed on the right way.
He keeps it on his shoulders, where it can't get away.
Which means he doesn't lose his head; it never goes astray.
And that, it seems, is more, much more, than most of us can say.

Ruth Ann

For the first time ever that anyone knew,
Ruth Ann was quiet.

Her father said, "You look down in the mouth.
Speak out dear, please try it."

Her best friend said, "Will a megaphone help?
Just tell me it will and I'll buy it."

Her brother said, "No, don't do that.
To me, this is a riot."

Her mother said, "Has the cat got your tongue?
With no tongue you'll have to diet."

But her bubblegum kept her mouth stuck tight,
So Ruth Ann stayed quiet.

Joan

Joan was puzzled by her father, Dale McBride,
Who said, every time she laughed with smile wide,
That she was "happy as a clam at high tide."

Joan decided that her father must be wrong,
For once at the beach as she walked along,
She'd heard a great big clam singing this song:

> To be a clam is not so easy
> And we clams are never happy at all
>
> When eating sand we get quite queasy
> We just seem to be having a ball.
>
> We're never really happy at all, at all,
> No, we clams are never happy at all.
>
> Being near the ocean breezy
> Makes us too cold to even crawl.
>
> You won't see us with smiles cheesy
> For clammy life is just too long a haul.
>
> We're never really happy at all, at all,
> No, we clams are never happy at all.
>
> To be a clam is not so easy
> And we clams are never happy at all.
>
> We're never really happy at all, at all,
> No, we clams are never happy at all.

Joan found the song to be an oddity,
Even when she heard it down by the sea.
And it did not a thing to explain her own glee.

Her smile had nothing to do with high tide,
It had grown by itself out of confidence and pride,
She found herself happy just being Joan McBride.

Would You?

Oh would you like to feel content?
Of course you would. It's evident
That pure content is heaven-sent.
But let me give you argument
That your content you could lament.
To be hog-wild may be your bent.
Content would then be detriment
Or feel like nasty punishment.
And is it really your intent
To give up tears and merriment
And feeling fresh or overspent?
If you like being vehement
Or joy of acting different
Or being scared out in a tent—
Don't wonder where such feelings went.
Don't be content to be content.

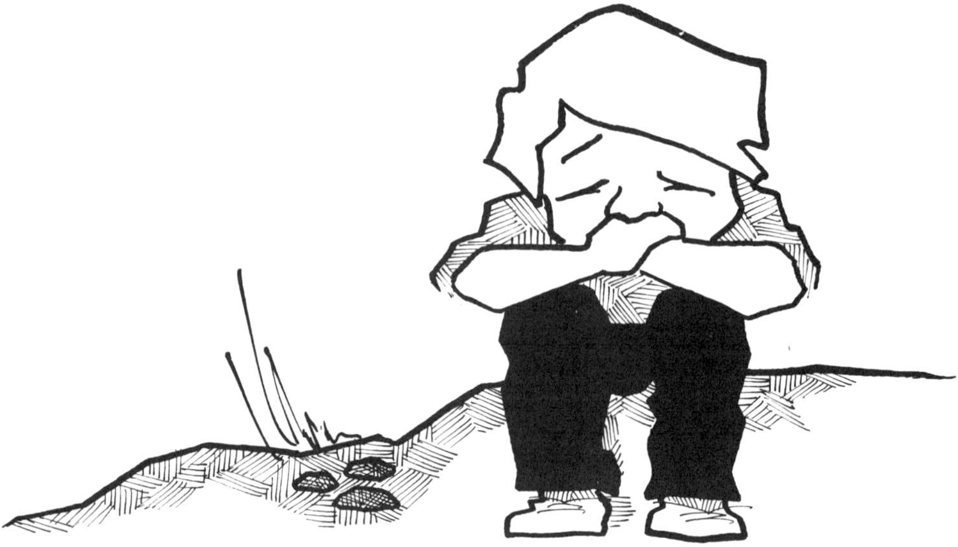

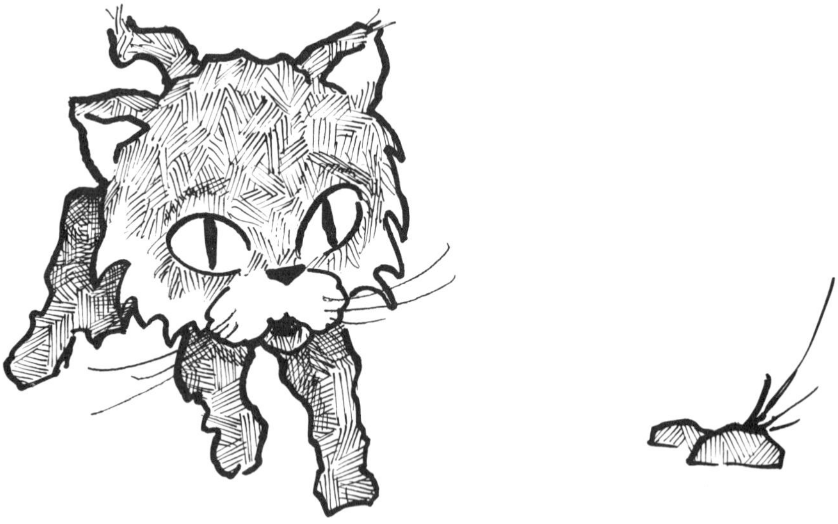

Hugh

When Hugh had just one jellybean
His friend Annie had fifteen
And sweet-toothed Hugh turned jealous green.

> In a backyard game of hide-and-seek
> Hugh hid so close and seemed so meek
> The other kids laughed at his yellow streak.

"Phooey, Hughie!" yelled cousin Ted.
Then angry Hugh began to see red
And bit his cousin in the head.

> Hugh's cat ran away, and his pet frog too.
> Poor Hugh grew blue so through and through
> That sitting and sniffing was all he could do.

When his multi-colored feelings came out of their cage
And Hugh could not control them—or even act his age—
He felt like many crayons mashed together on a page.

> But when all the feelings settled down from head to toe
> When his insides were bubbly, and his smile began to grow
> Then Hugh looked and felt like his own rainbow.

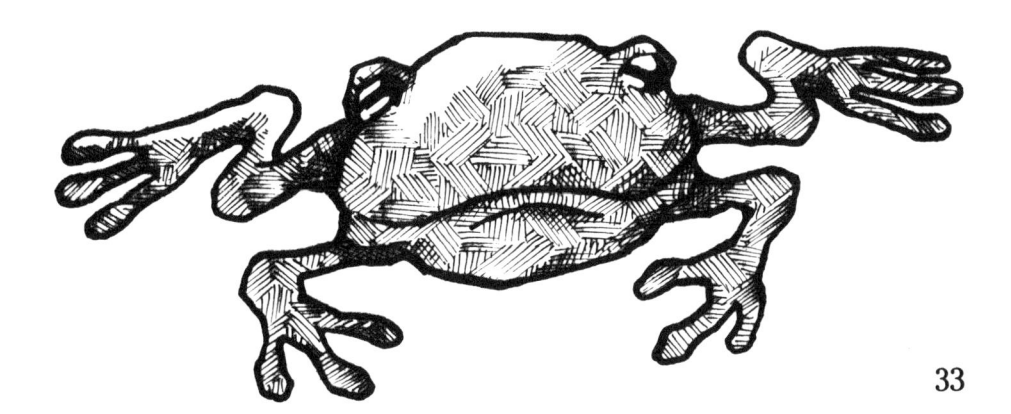

Wrong

Did you ever try
To get up
On the wrong side of bed?
Probably you hit a wall.
Maybe you had a fall.
No wonder you were grumpy.

Bob

Bob wished to do both this and that, and be both here and there.
It seemed that making a decision was more than he could bear.
So first he chewed his fingernails, and next he pulled his hair,
And then he went in circles that did not go anywhere.

Lucille and Neal

"How do you feel?" said Lucille to Neal.
"I'm hungry," he said. "I feel like a meal."
"That's silly," she answered, "and not very real.
You don't look like a fish or potatoes or veal.
I think as a meal you lack all appeal."
"I guess you are right," said Neal to Lucille,
"I guess it is not like a meal that I feel.
I just feel like a ride in an automobile."

Joe

There came a day that Joe was feeling sore.
His feelings had been hurt right to the core,
By Jim, who'd said that Joe was really numb,
That nobody on earth could be so dumb.

Joe tried to take his feelings out on Bess,
Until he saw her evident distress.
He said he had not wished to make her cry—
In fact that made him so sad he could die.

"Oh don't do that," she said, "Oh please don't go!
But do tell me one thing I need to know—
Just why are you so mean to me
When you say you don't mean to be?"

"I've tried, I think," he said, "to make you take
All the hurtful things that make me ache.
But what I tried has happened in reverse.
When I give you bad feelings, I myself feel worse."

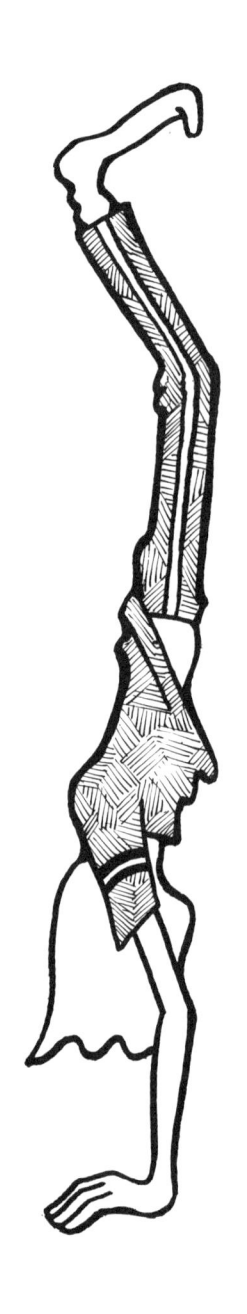

Sam

They said Sam was hyper, and maybe he was—
He sometimes did handstands without any cause.
But something about that might give us all pause,
For the handstands he did, he did without flaws.

Annie

Why did Annie end her pout
And why did Annie start to grin
When her friend Kenneth left no doubt
He wished to take her for a spin?

To Annie that's what life was about,
For she had reached the strange age when
Just staying in meant being left out
And going out meant being in.

Cindy Lou

Young Cindy Lou was sometimes two when one would do.

She found herself beside herself when faced with rage or glee.
Instead of shouting angrily—or saying, "Hey!" or "Gee!"
Or singing happy sounds just like a chickadee,
She split herself in two—into her own small family.

Poor Cindy Lou who once was one but now was two.

She tried while still beside herself to calm her inner roar,
Then spied her selves reflected in the mirror on the door,
And saw with shock that now she had turned into four.
"One Cindy Lou is all we need," she said, "not more."

How sad but true, this Cindy Lou was not just one but two times two.

To be her own quartet was more than she had planned,
If she kept up she would become a band—
A geekish freak, the worst in any land.
The time had come, she knew, to take herself in hand.

To see herself not one but few was too, too much for Cindy Lou.

She reached right out and gave herself a hug,
And pulled herself together with a good firm tug.
She found that this was easy—she did it with a shrug.
And got her selves inside herself, all safe and warm and snug.

She grew from two times two to one—Smart Cindy Lou!

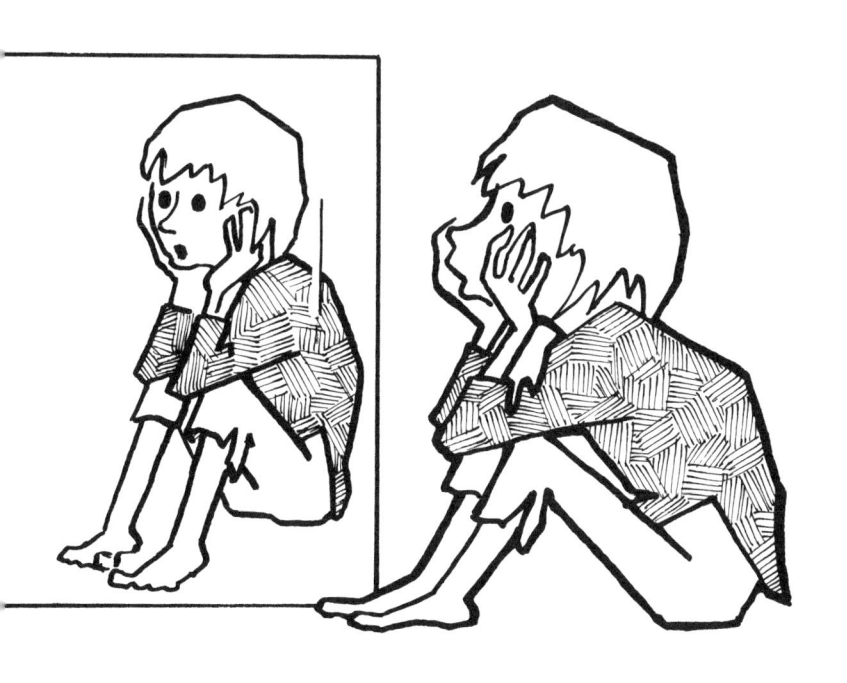

How Far?

How far can feelings go?
As far, my friend, as from me to you,
And from you to me and back
Is as far as feelings can go.

    As far as is
    And as far as can be
    And as far as was
    Is as far as feelings can go.

As far as around
And as far as within
Is as far as feelings can go,
My friend.

Barnaby

The frog in his throat
Got Barnaby's goat.
He had this to say
When they both went away:
"Those two were a crowd
For crying out loud."

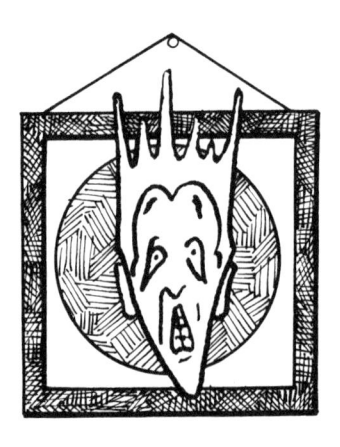

Feelingmore Pharr

You might think you're ugly,
And maybe you are.
But you're not as ugly
As Feelingmore Pharr.
He's the ugliest kid in the world.

How would you look
If your teeth were on edge
Or your hair stood up straight
Whenever you felt afraid?
You would look like Feelingmore Pharr.

How would you look
If when you grew sad
Your face began to grow long?
How would you look
If you were called "lazy bones"
And you were, so
Your limbs always drooped
When you felt pooped?
You would look like Feelingmore Pharr.

How would you look
If when you laughed
You split your sides
Then tried to pull
Yourself together?
You would look like Feelingmore Pharr.

How would you look
With a foot in your mouth
Or your nose out of joint
Or being all thumbs
Or all eyes?
You would look like Feelingmore Pharr.

You might think you're ugly,
And maybe you are.
But you're not as ugly
As Feelingmore Pharr.
He's the ugliest kid in the world.
By far.

Sid

Sid was so tightly tongue-tied
That his father groaned and deep-sighed
While his mother moaned and "oh-my'd"
And both looked at him wide-eyed.

Sid's tongue stayed tied up in a bow
Until he pulled one end and lo!
His thoughts came in such copious flow
His parents cried, "Oh, whoa, Oh woe."

But he kept on, and finally snapped,
"You treated me as handicapped,
When I just had my feelings trapped.
You should have seen me as gift-wrapped."

Whittington

Whittington Harrison May
Was often a handful of boy.
Once on a long boring day
Whit burned his sister's best toy
Then laughed at his fiery prank.
His mother made use of her knee
To give the young handful a spank
And quiet his cackling glee.
"It pains me to do this my son,"
She said as she caused him to bend,
"But I so dislike what you've done,
That I have arrived at wits' end."

Andrea

Feelings are like tiny seeds.
They can turn into ugly weeds
Or into lovely colored flowers
With blooms that last for many hours.

Andrea found this out and squealed,
"My feelings have become a field."
And then she took a funny chance—
She picked all of her feeling plants.

She threw them into her bathtub,
Then jumped in too, to think and scrub.
When she was done she finally knew
What it means to sit and stew.

David Lee

David Lee was told as sternly as could be,
That he was being nasty as could be.
And then was told as quickly as could be,
That Ruth was angry as could be,
That Tim was surly as could be,
That Joan was grouchy as could be,
And Al was sassy as could be.
So Dave was puzzled as could be.
He wondered who this Koodbe kid could be.

50

Ed

Everybody, everybody else, it seemed to Ed,
Had a closest friend—even stupid Fred.
But Ed had just plain old simple friends instead,
And his need for a best friend was a pain in his head.

When Ed thought about his friends, he saw each had a lack—
Some gave too much foolishness, and some gave too much flack.
In finding all their weaknesses, Ed found he had a knack,
So as best friends he gave each plain old friend the sack.

Eventually Ed also gave each friend he had a letter grade
Based on the stuff of which best friends are made—
To ask you swimming, even if they know you only wade,
To put you on their team for any game that's played.

Anne, who danced with him, but poorly, got a C.
And Tom, who ran too fast for Ed, received a D.
While Beth, who laughed at his plump stomach, got an E.
But Chris, who shared his candy, got a B.

"Hey, Ed," said a friend, who just happened Ed's way,
"You may wait for perfection till your very last day.
It's not up to us to earn your grade A.
The challenge is for you to give it away.

"I know what is wrong, and I'll make you a bet,
You don't want a closest friend, you just want a pet,
You judge any friendship by what you will get,
And in that, my friend, I think you're all wet."

Ed listened very closely, and he finally got the clue,
That if making close friends was what he wished to do,
Then making harsh judgements was completely taboo—
For to have a good friend you must be one, too.

Abigail

When Abigail Rodgers fell for Brett,
She wound up feeling quite upset.
When she got a crush on Art,
It almost broke her own sweet heart.
And so she failed to understand,
Why people say that love is grand.

R. Larson Brown

R. Larson Brown based all his fears and hopes
On what he found in daily horoscopes.
One day they said to watch his step, and so
He kept his eyes glued to each sneaker's toe.
He did not even know a cyclone was around
Until it roared on in and yanked him from the ground.

Are fates and feelings really written in the stars?
To know, I guess, we'll have to wait for Lars.
When he comes dropping back to us, through the stiller air,
Perhaps he'll let us know what he has read up there.
But I'll believe, until I get such proof,
That fate and feelings are controlled beneath my roof.

Pamela and Frank

Pamela Whidby loved to love. She also hated to hate,
Until she mentioned her feelings to Frank.

> "How boring," he said. "No wonder you're so very dull.
> You should follow my example and turn your feelings around.
> Try hating to love and loving to hate, just the way I do."

Pamela tried Frank's way, but she could not make it work.
When she struggled very hard to hate love, her love faded away.
Then she had no love to use for loving hate.
"This simply will not work," she said.

> "But you're just getting started," argued Frank.
> "When you hate to love and love to hate
> There are all sorts of things to be done.
> Let's go out and kick some kids
> Then scream when they fight back.
> That's what I always do."

"No," said Pamela. "You are utterly, completely wrong.
Nobody can really love hate and really hate love.
But you can be afraid of both hate and love, and I think you are.
You try to keep both of them out so you won't feel either.
Then you get empty inside, so you fill yourself with trouble."

> Pamela went back to loving love and hating hate.
> She felt like herself again, and was glad.

And Frank? Frank went off to think.

A Physical Feeling

A physical feeling
That's fun to have—
Are you ready for this?
Is a sneeze.
You might think it's drippy
Or otherwise bad.
But I say it's fun,
If you please.
It can be a surprise
Right under your eyes
And I have a friend who agrees.
A sneeze can be nice
If it comes once or twice
And it comes all alone with no wheeze.
It starts with a tickle
That turns to an itch
And when it explodes
It's a breeze.
But don't take it lightly,
It might be unsightly
And could even mean
A disease.
My friend also says
It is nothing to sneeze at,
But I think he says that
To tease.

Sue

In a circle of friends, Sue said to Joe, "I think that Lance is a so-and-so." Joe told Fred and Fred told Flo. And so... and so, the word moved on, from Flo to Jane to Anne and Don. At first it seemed like just a joke. But when Don told Lance then the circle broke.

57

Mortimer Sharp

Mortimer Sharp was on pins and needles.
He worried about everything under the sun.
"Just relax," his mother said,
"And take things as they come."
He tried and tried, but failed and said,
"Instead I think I'll get some metal shoes.
That will be the thimble thing to do."

Laurie

Laurie puffed out her cheeks
To fill a balloon with her love.
It lifted her up then, up to the sky
Until she was high as a kite.
She floated along for a wonderful time,
And landed on top of the world.

What Can You Do?

What can you do with feelings
        That you wish you didn't have?
You can't stick them in the garbage
        And slam the cover on.
You can't beat them up
        Without hurting yourself.
But you might get them out through your mouth
        By shouting them away
        (If nobody minds the noise).
Or you can talk them out quite quietly
        If you can find a friend.
Or you can take them on a ride.
        Bad feelings always fall off
        Fast moving bicycles.
Or you can make them go fly a kite.
        Bad feelings fall off kites, too.
Or you can use a double-death-dealing-
        Anti-bad-feeling drug
        Called thought and understanding.
That's what you can do with feelings
        That you wish you didn't have.

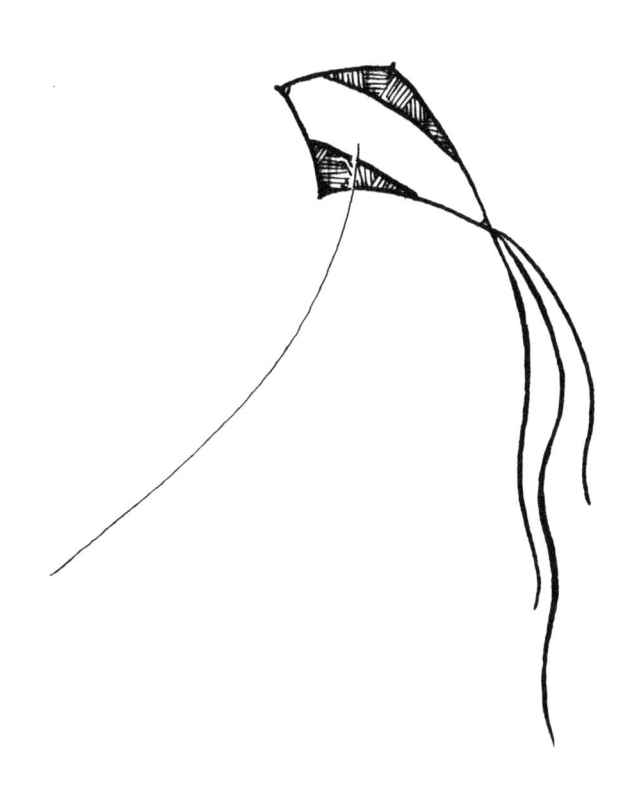

MAR 2005